Great Smoky Mountains National Park

John Hamilton

Published by ABDO Publishing Company, 4940 Viking Drive, Suite 622, Edina, Minnesota 55435.

Printed in the United States.

Editor: Paul Joseph

Graphic Design: John Hamilton

All photos and illustrations by John Hamilton, except National Park Service, p. 16 (musicians), p. 17 (park map), p. 21 (black bear).

Library of Congress Cataloging-in-Publication Data

Hamilton, John, 1959–
    Great Smoky Mountains National Park / John Hamilton.
       p. cm. — (National parks)
    Includes index.
    ISBN 1-59197-943-9
    1. Great Smoky Mountains National Park (N.C. and Tenn.)—Juvenile literature. I. Title.
II. National parks (ABDO Publishing Company)

    F443.G7H33 2005
    976.8'89—dc22
                          2004055433

Contents

A moss-covered tree stump found along the Roaring Fork Motor Nature Trail.

Grotto Falls can be found after a short walk through a hemlock forest.

Land of Diversity

Great Smoky Mountains National Park is a land of contrasts. It is a place where human history and natural history collide, creating a park that is part wilderness and part museum, part bio-preserve and part recreation center.

Located about 25 miles (40 km) south of Knoxville, Tennessee, Great Smoky is nestled within the southern end of the Appalachian Mountains, perched on the border between North Carolina and Tennessee. It contains about 800 square miles (2,072 sq km) of mountain landscape, home to an incredible variety of trees, wildflowers, and animals. But to get here you first must travel through a maze of commercial development, including the many hotels, shopping malls, and amusement centers which ring the outside of the park.

The north entrance is the park's most popular. The first hint of wilderness comes after leaving busy Pigeon Forge, Tennessee. A winding road leads uphill. Tall trees grow on either side of the highway, their thick overhanging canopy shielding the sunlight and painting everything below in shades of green. Just when you think you've left the last neon sign of civilization behind, you enter Gatlinburg, Tennessee, a tourist playground that hums with activity.

After passing through the crowded resort town, you finally cross the park boundary. The transformation is startling. Suddenly you're transported into a forested wilderness that seems as old as the hills. Great forests wrap their shoulders around mist-shrouded mountain ridges. Gnarled tree roots entangle and merge with boulders covered in emerald-colored sheets of moss. The air has a humid, fragrant smell. In spring and summer, wildflowers punctuate the green landscape with dots of pink, white, yellow, and purple. In autumn, the hardwood forests of the valleys and coves change their leaves, setting the hills ablaze in a riot of color. Babbling mountain streams, many crowded with fish and salamanders, cascade over boulder-strewn hillsides or through valleys teeming with wildlife.

Great Smoky Mountains National Park is one of the biggest park preserves in the eastern United States. There are more tree species here than in all of Northern Europe. More than 1,500 flowering plants dot the park's ridge-like mountains and lush valleys. Sixty mammal species and dozens of native fish make the park their home. Overhead, more than 200 species of birds take flight in the misty skies.

The ancient ridges of Great Smoky Mountains are some of the oldest mountains in the world, and some of the highest in the eastern United States. Twelve peaks in the park tower more than 6,000 feet (1,829 m) in altitude. Different ecosystems can be found as one travels up and down the park's varied terrain. Because of the many different habitats, from the spruce-fir forests of the higher elevations to the pine-and-oak woodlands of the drier lower slopes, a rich variety of plants and wildlife can be found in this single park.

Great Smoky Mountains is so well known for its biological diversity that it has been designated an International Biosphere Reserve. The mission of the National Park Service is to protect this rich mixture of plants and wildlife for visitors today and for future generations.

More than nine million people visit Great Smoky Mountains each year, the most of any national park. To discover all the different sights for themselves, visitors can hike on more than 800 miles (1,287 km) of marked trails, many of them passing through ancient old-growth forests. More than 380 miles (612 km) of roads also pass through the park.

Great Smoky Mountains National Park is known for more than just its mountain scenery, plants, and wildlife. It also contains a mix of the natural world and early human settlement. Preserved within the park are old-fashioned cabins, churches, mills, and farms, forming a unique snapshot of how Southern Appalachian mountain people once lived.

The Great Smoky Mountains are often seen shrouded in mist, especially on humid summer mornings or evenings. Cherokee Indians, who once called the park their home, described the mountains as shaconage. It is a word that means "blue, like smoke."

Ninety-five percent of the park is covered in woodlands, and 25 percent of that is old-growth forest. So much of the foliage is so tightly packed that the water and hydrocarbons from the air-breathing leaves can be seen as a filmy "smoke" that settles on the landscape.

"Time has lingered in Appalachia."—Horace Kephart

Smoky Mountain Geology

A spine of mountain peaks forms the central part of Great Smoky Mountains National Park, running roughly southwest and northeast and marking the border between North Carolina and Tennessee. Jutting out from this dividing line are ridges of lower-elevation hills that seem to recede off into the distance, oftentimes shrouded in mist or clouds.

The Great Smoky Mountains were formed between 200 and 300 million years ago. They are among the oldest mountains on the planet. The volcanic granite and gneiss bedrock underneath them is at least one billion years old. On top of the bedrock are hundreds of millions of years' worth of accumulated sedimentary rock, the result of the area being underneath a shallow sea.

Long ago, two continental plates collided over a period of millions of years, pushing up the mountains we know today as the Appalachians. The Great Smoky Mountains are on the southern end of this mountain chain.

When they were first formed, the Smokies were much more rugged and higher in elevation than they are now. They were more like the Rocky Mountains of western North America. Millions of years of erosion by rain, wind, ice, and vegetation have worn the Smokies down into the smooth layers of forest-covered mountain ridges that we see today.

A tumbling **mountain stream** cuts through ancient rock.

Diversity of Life

When most people, especially biologists, think of the Great Smoky Mountains, they think of the tremendous diversity of plants and animals found in the park. There are only about 800 square miles (2,072 sq km) of parkland preserved here, a relatively small area. But packed inside the park boundaries are more than 10,000 living species. Some scientists think there may be another 90,000 species waiting to be discovered. There isn't another temperate-climate landscape of equal size in the world that can match this amazing richness of life. Why is there such diversity here?

One reason is the different altitudes found inside the park, which range from 875 to 6,643 feet (267 to 2,025 m) above sea level. The weather is much different at the higher elevations than it is in the park's valleys and coves. Different altitudes support different kinds of plants and animals. It's like traveling from a northern state like Maine all the way south to Georgia.

Secondly, the last ice age, which occurred about 10,00 years ago, didn't quite make it as far south as the Great Smoky Mountains. But northern-climate animals and plants were pushed south into the area. When the glaciers finally retreated, many of these species remained along the spine of the higher-elevation mountains.

Weather is a third factor that adds to the park's diversity. Annual rainfall varies from about 55 inches (140 cm) in the lowlands to more than 85 inches (216 cm) on some mountaintops. This is more rain than anywhere else in the country except the Pacific Northwest. This abundant rainfall, plus high summertime humidity, helps many kinds of plants to grow.

There are more than 5,000 kinds of plants in Great Smoky Mountains National Park.

About 100 species of trees grow in the Smokies. That's more than in any other national park in North America. More than 5,000 kinds of plants, both flowering and non-flowering, can be found within the park. Colorful rhododendrons and mountain laurels are especially popular with park visitors.

Many animal species have had thousands of years of isolation inside the park in which to branch out and diversify. There are 30 species of salamanders here, making Great Smoky Mountains National Park the "Salamander Capital of the World." The park is also well known among biologists for its diverse species of mollusks, millipedes, and mushrooms.

Human History in the Park

When white settlers first entered the Great Smoky Mountains in the 1700s, they found the area already inhabited by Cherokee Indians. The Cherokee people had been in the Smokies since about 1,000 A.D., when they formed villages throughout their nation. For hundreds of years the Indians used old bison trails over the mountains to do trade with neighboring tribes. The Cherokee had a deep love and knowledge of the land and its plants and wildlife.

By the late 1700's, Americans of European descent began pushing westward. Armed clashes with the Cherokee, in addition to new diseases, forced the Indians to compromise and adapt to the newcomers' way of life. Cherokee chiefs signed treaties with the United States government, giving away most of their land in the Smokies. White settlers from Kentucky, Virginia, and North Carolina streamed into the lowland areas, starting new farms and building cabins. But there wasn't enough land for all the new settlers. They also wanted the remaining lands occupied by the Cherokee.

In 1838, President Andrew Jackson ordered the removal of the Indians. In the Cherokee Nations' darkest hour, they were rounded up and forced to move to reservations in far-away Oklahoma. The trip would become known as the "Trail of Tears." Some Indians defied the government and hid in secluded areas of the Smokies. Today some of their descendents live on the Qualla Reservation, which borders the southern part of Smoky Mountains National Park in North Carolina.

The two-story house built by Noah "Bud" Ogle (above) is on a farm started by Ogle and his family in 1879. Many farms were located near streams to take advantage of running water. This flume (below) transports water to a mill near the Ogle farm.

By the mid 1800's, white settlers had established themselves in several areas of the Smoky Mountains, especially in fertile bottomlands like Roaring Fork Valley, Cades Cove, and White Oak Flats (which would later become Gatlinburg, Tennessee).

Mountain living was very basic. After clearing land, settlers planted fields of corn. Deer, bear, and squirrel were hunted in the woods, and fish were caught in the rivers. Almost every one-room log cabin had a garden planted next to it. Most of life's necessities were made by the mountain folk themselves. Corn was ground up at mills constructed on the shores of swift-moving streams. Honey and apples were important cash crops.

By the late 1800's, loggers took notice of the Appalachian hardwood forests. By 1920, almost two-thirds of the land now enclosed by the national park was cut down or burned by forest fire.

Alarmed at the rapid loss of this unique landscape, many people pleaded with the government to preserve what was left of the area. Horace Kephart, a local librarian, was very influential in the preservation movement. "Why," he asked, "should future generations be robbed of all chance to see with their own eyes what a real forest… is like?"

In 1926, the U.S. government approved the park. The next eight years were spent buying up thousands of parcels of privately owned land. Most of the mountain folk left their homes, although many buildings were preserved by the National Park Service so that visitors could see how people once lived in the early days.

In 1934, Great Smoky Mountains National Park was finally established, preserving this unique mountain landscape for future generations.

Reenactors perform bluegrass music on the porch of a restored cabin in the park.

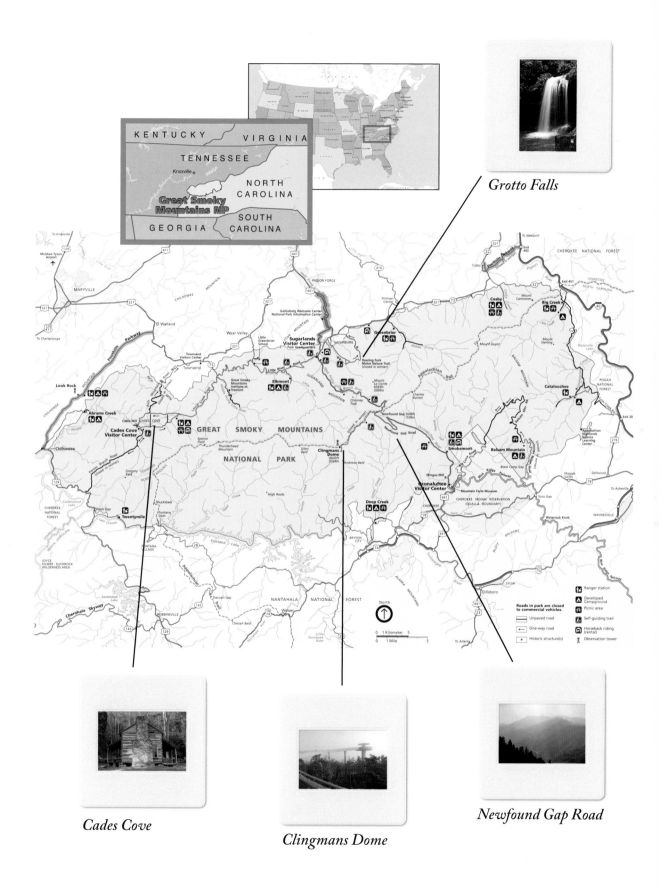

Grotto Falls

Cades Cove

Clingmans Dome

Newfound Gap Road

17

Fall colors light up Cades Cove (above). An ancient tree wraps its root around a moss-covered boulder (below) near the Noah "Bud" Ogle farm.

Many people come to Great Smoky Mountains in September and October to admire the autumn colors (above). A herd of horses (below) grazes in a field near Cades Cove.

Animals in the Park

Great Smoky Mountains National Park is one of the largest protected wilderness areas in the eastern United States. It provides a sanctuary to many kinds of animals, some of them endangered. Protected within the park are more than 50 species of mammals, 200 species of birds, and 50 native fish species. In addition, more than 80 kinds of reptiles and amphibians can be found here.

The park is probably most famous for its population of American black bear. Biologists estimate that there are approximately 1,500 black bears living here, almost two bears for every square mile in the park.

White-tailed deer are also plentiful in the park. Both deer and bear are hard for visitors to spot. The dense forests of the park give many animals good cover in which to hide. In the park's more open areas, like Cades Cove, bear and deer sightings are very common.

In the park's cooler elevations, usually above 4,500 feet (1,377 m), red squirrel, red fox, grouse, ravens, and chickadee are commonly found. In the lower woodlands, valleys, and coves, you are more likely to find white-tailed deer, black bear, box turtles, barred owls, wild turkey, chipmunks, and even an occasional bobcat. Various kinds of salamanders and bats can be found throughout the park.

The bark on this tree trunk shows marks made by bear claws.

Great Smoky Mountains National Park is famous for its population of black bear (above), which are easiest to spot in coves and other areas cleared of heavy vegetation. Chipmunks (below) are very common in pine-and-oak forests.

Forest Types

Great Smoky Mountains National Park doesn't have the jaw-dropping natural scenery of a Yellowstone or Yosemite. And the animals found here hardly justify national park status. What really makes Smoky Mountains special is a mind-boggling variety of plants. The vegetation here really is extraordinary, with 100 native tree species and over 100 different kinds of shrubs. Wildflowers, ferns, and mosses are also found here in rich varieties.

The park's vegetation grows in five distinct forest types. On dry, lower-elevation slopes that are exposed to direct sunlight, pine-and-oak forests grow. Rhododendron and mountain laurel thickets, hickory, and flowering dogwood trees are also found here.

Hemlock forests dominate the shadier lower elevations. They are also common on the shores of rivers and streams. Hemlock trees were cut in pioneer days for their tannin-rich bark, which was used to tan leather.

Sheltered valleys with deep, rich soil are called coves. Cove hardwood forests that are found here, up to an elevation of about 4,500 feet (1,372 m), include yellow birch, Carolina silverbell, sugar maple, hickory, and beech trees.

Northern hardwood forests are broadleaved trees that are adapted to higher elevations, usually above 4,500 feet (1,372 m). These forests mainly include beech and yellow birch trees, with some maple, basswood, and yellow buckeye.

Growing on the highest mountains of the park are the spruce-fir forests. These evergreens mainly include Fraser fir and red spruce. Large treeless meadows are called balds, and may be covered with shrubs or flowers such as rhododendron, mountain laurel, and azaleas.

Cades Cove (above) contains typical hardwoods such as yellow birch, sugar maple, and hickory. Hemlock forests (below) are found in lower elevations with lots of shade.

Park Highlights

About nine million people visit Great Smoky Mountains National Park each year. The most popular times to visit are in the summer and the autumn, when tree leaves are changing color. During these times park roads can be very crowded, making for a very unpleasant experience.

Luckily, there's a way to escape the crowds and recapture the feeling of unspoiled wilderness: park the car and get out and hike. Besides the hundreds of miles of established trails, the park has Quiet Walkways, quarter-mile (.4 km) groomed paths built off the main roads. Signs marking the trails call them "a little bit of the world as it once was." Many of the trails in the park are lightly used, even during peak tourist season. Most tourists prefer to visit strictly from the comfort of their vehicles.

Newfound Gap Road runs northwest and southeast, connecting the two big visitor centers on the northern and southern ends of the park. The winding road starts about 2,000 feet (610 m) above sea level, then slowly climbs all the way up across the spine of the Smoky Mountains. There are several tunnels and mountain overlooks that make this an exciting ride.

Many old structures in the park, like this farm house in Cades Cove, have been preserved.

Three backpackers (above) start their journey at Clingmans Dome, the highest spot in the park. Nearby is a connection to the Appalachian Trail, which runs east and west through Great Smoky Mountains. Many park trails lead to streams and waterfalls (below).

As the road rises, you pass through different kinds of forests, from the hardwood timbers of the lowlands to the spruce-fir forests of the higher elevations. Rain or fog can be encountered on almost any day, especially at the tops of the mountain peaks, even when the day seems bright and sunny at the lower elevations. There are many places along the road to stop your car and hike into the forests.

Some trails, especially along the Roaring Fork Motor Nature Trail near Gatlinburg, Tennessee, take you to magnificent waterfalls. The park is famous for its cascading streams. Other off-the-beaten-path areas include Balsam Mountain Road and Cataloochee in the southeastern part of the park. Elk have been reintroduced at Cataloochee, and can often be spotted in clearings.

A few miles off Newfound Gap Road, at the top of the Smoky Mountains, is Clingmans Dome. At 6,643 feet (2,025 m), it is the highest spot in the park. A short half-mile (.8 km) trail leads to a concrete lookout tower. The panoramic views from the tower can be magnificent, even on cloudy days. A young boy one summer morning, as part of a school field trip, came running up the winding ramp, then gripped the handrail and peered out over the mountaintops, his eyes wide. "We're on top of the world!" the boy shouted to his classmates.

Cades Cove, in the northwestern edge of the park, is one of the most popular spots in Great Smokies. An 11-mile (18-km) loop road travels through this high valley, which was heavily settled in the 1800s. There are many structures left behind to explore, including pioneer cabins, churches, farms, and mills. Because Cades Cove has many open areas, it is easy to spot deer, black bear, and other wildlife, especially at dawn or dusk.

The tower at Clingmans Dome is a popular spot for school groups to learn more about the park.

The Primitive Baptist Church (above) was started by Cades Cove residents in 1827. The current frame building was built in 1887. The burial ground is the final resting place for many early cove families. The tower at Clingmans Dome (below) is the highest spot in the park.

Future Challenges

Despite its protection as a national park, there are many threats to the Great Smoky Mountains. Most of them are created by the actions of humans. Overcrowding and pollution has impacted park ecosystems in ways that scientists are trying to better understand.

In the last several decades visibility in the park has been greatly reduced because of man-made air pollution, either from automobiles or nearby cities. Microscopic sulfate particles from air pollution add to the mountains' natural haze. Since the 1950's visibility from scenic viewpoints has been reduced about 80 percent in the summer months. Air pollution also hurts the park's trees, especially red spruce. Ozone pollution and acid rain are other threats. Nearby power-generating plants have installed equipment in recent years to reduce their ozone- and haze-causing emissions, but air quality is still a persistent problem.

Insect pests introduced from Europe and Asia have endangered many of the park's trees. Woolly adelgid, gypsy moths, and southern pine beetles threaten to devastate the area's Fraser firs, hemlock, and other hardwood forests. In addition to killing these pests with insecticides, park officials are releasing predator beetles, especially to battle woolly adelgid.

There are many reasons to be hopeful that the threats to Great Smoky Mountains National Park will be reduced or eliminated in coming years. But it will take constant alertness by the National Park Service, as well as the help of an educated public.

It's well worth the effort to preserve this special place. Each new generation has the right to experience what it's like to stroll through an unspoiled wilderness. As one young boy said to his father as they hiked hand-in-hand through an old-growth forest, "Dad, I'm really pleased to be here."

Although most of the park's many streams and rivers (above) remain free of chemical pollutants, acid rain and waterborne diseases like giardia threaten water quality. Pests and disease also threaten Great Smoky Mountains' many forest ecosystems (below).

Glossary

CONTINENTAL DIVIDE

A ridge of the Rocky Mountains in North America. Water flowing east of the divide eventually goes to the Atlantic Ocean. Water flowing west goes to the Pacific Ocean.

ECOSYSTEM

A biological community of animals, plants, and bacteria, all of whom live together in the same physical or chemical environment.

FEDERAL LANDS

Much of America's land, especially in the western part of the country, is maintained by the United States federal government. These are public lands owned by all U.S. citizens. There are many kinds of federal lands. National parks, like Great Smoky Mountains, are federal lands that are set aside so that they can be preserved. Other federal lands, such as national forests or national grasslands, are used in many different ways, including logging, ranching, and mining. Much of the land surrounding Great Smoky Mountains National Park is maintained by the government, including several national forests and wildlife refuges.

FOREST SERVICE

The United States Department of Agriculture (USDA) Forest Service was started in 1905 to manage public lands in national forests and grasslands. The Forest Service today oversees an area of 191 million acres (77.3 million hectares), which is an amount of land about the same size as Texas. In addition to protecting and managing America's public lands, the Forest Service also conducts forestry research and helps many state government and private forestry programs.

GEOLOGICAL SURVEY

The United States Geological Survey was created in 1879. It is an independent science agency that is part of the Department of the Interior. It researches and collects facts about the land of the United States, giving us a better understanding of our natural resources.

GLACIER

A glacier is often called a river of ice. It is made of thick sheets of ice and snow. Glaciers slowly move downhill, scouring and smoothing the landscape.

TEMPERATE ZONE

A moderate climate zone that is found between the tropics and the polar circles.

Mushrooms growing on a moss-covered tree trunk in a hemlock forest.

Index